Waifus and Husbandos Coloring Book

Volume One

by ANGEL.FANART

Dedication

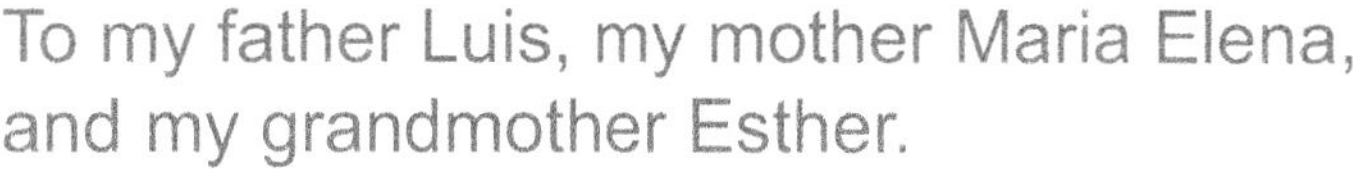

To my father Luis, my mother Maria Elena, and my grandmother Esther.

You gave me the best education and values, and supported me through this challenging artistic journey. Your unwavering encouragement has always been my source of strength and inspiration.

Thank you for believing in me and for your endless support. I love you all very much.

Angel Manrique

Let's Get Started

My name is Angel Manrique, and I am a self-taught artist from Peru. I come from a humble family rich in values, which has deeply inspired my artistic journey.

For over five years, I have honed my digital drawing style focused on anime, using my iPad and the Ibispaint app. Additionally, I am exploring and learning the art of semi-realistic style, always seeking new ways to improve and expand my art.

This book is the first edition of a series that I hope you enjoy. It is a collection of my favorite works, designed for you to enjoy coloring and adding your personal touch to each drawing.

If you want to see the fully colored versions of these drawings for reference, you can find them on my Instagram account: @angel.fanart.

My dream is for my art to be seen and appreciated by many people around the world, and to inspire others to follow their passions, no matter the circumstances.

I hope you enjoy this journey of color and creativity as much as I enjoyed creating it. Thank you for being part of my dream and for allowing my art to be a part of your life!

With love and gratitude,

ANGEL.FANART

Coloring Instructions

Before you start coloring, it is important to follow these instructions for a clean and detailed result:

Know the Character:

Before you start coloring, make sure to know the character you are coloring. Research their appearance and personality to capture their essence in your coloring. You can find the fully colored versions of these illustrations on my Instagram account @angel.fanart for reference.

Prepare Your Workspace:

Make sure to have a clean and well-lit workspace. Use good quality coloring materials such as colored pencils, markers, or watercolors for better results.

Clean and Detailed Coloring:

Use soft, controlled strokes to color each area. You can start with light layers and then add more color to create shadows and depth.

Use different coloring techniques, such as blending, stippling, or gradient, to add texture and realism to your work.

Pay attention to details and work patiently to achieve a clean and detailed coloring.

With these instructions, you will be ready to start coloring and bringing your favorite anime characters to life.

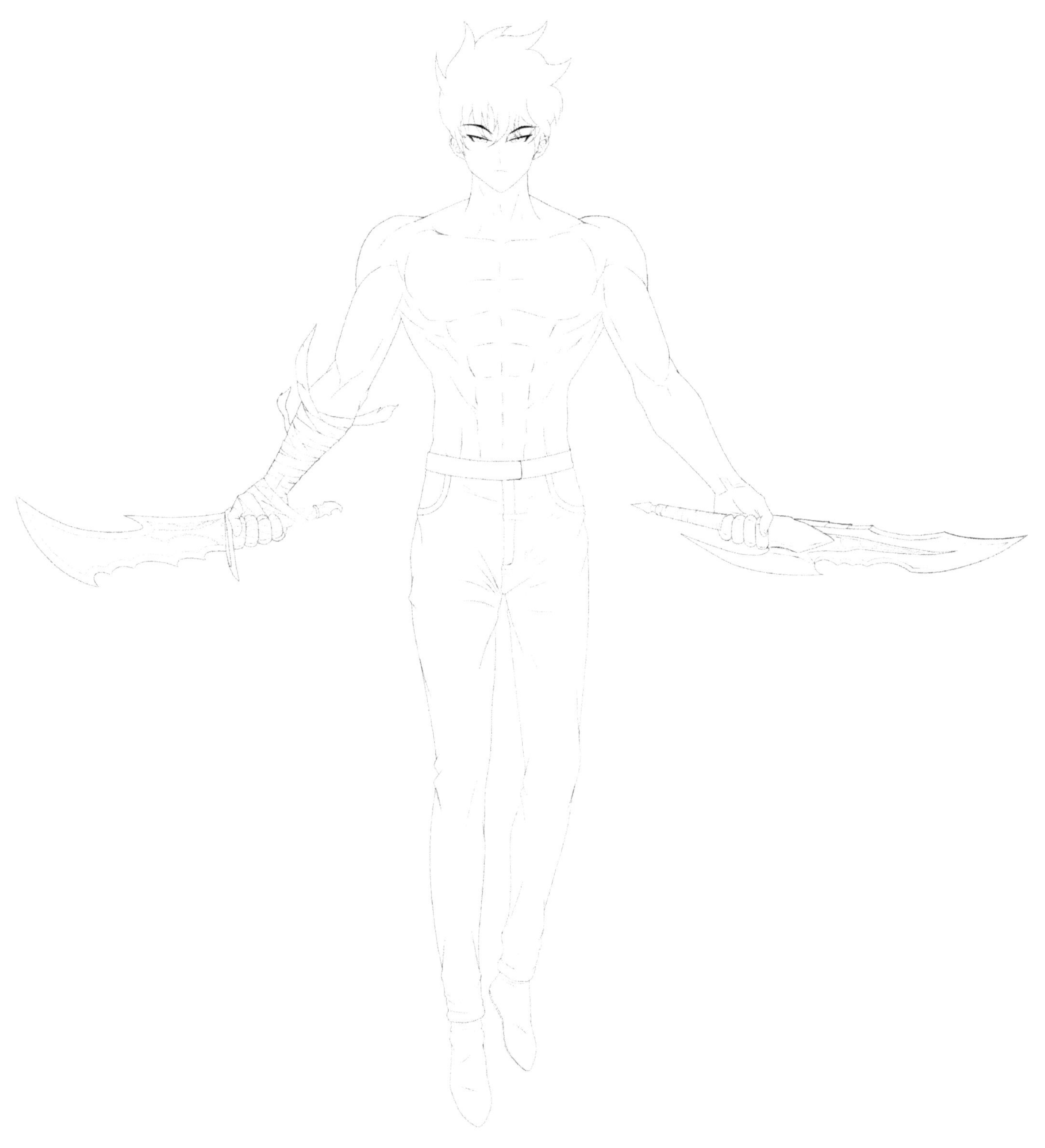

Sung Jin woo

Bunny Suit N18

Yor

Midnight

Zoro

Monkey D Luffy

Yuzuriha

Shikimori

Mirko

Itsuki Nakano

Bunny suit Fern

Rampage Gabimaru

Mitsuri Kanroji

OC Vivian of Anifigure
Club n' Angelfanart

Lucy

Dragon Warrior Zero Two

Nino Nakano

Rias Gremory on lingerie

www.ingramcontent.com/pod-product-compliance
Lightning Source LLC
Chambersburg PA
CBHW081603250726
48653CB00009B/3546